AF444549

Dog Food Cookbook

Easy and Healthy Recipes for Your Pet

Catalina Morris

Table of Contents

CHAPTER FIVE

CHAPTER SIX

CHAPTER SEVEN

Introduction

Dogs are dear friends and family members. We want our dogs to have a perfect life, and food is a big part. It's no secret that dogs love to eat pretty much anything that comes their way. From clothes to chair legs, there is no way of knowing what your precious fur buddy will see as a delicious meal or chew toy. However, on the human side of the relationship, we have the responsibility to make sure that our dogs have a healthy diet, one that's tailored to fit their needs.

Dog food comes in many shapes, forms, and flavors. The kibbles and wet food that we give our dogs claim to contain all the vitamins, minerals, and nutrients that a pooch could ever need to grow healthy and strong. There's no mistake that some dog food brands are fully committed to delivering on this promise. You can usually tell by the price point which food is quality and which is a dog equivalent of fast food. Most dog treats, for example, are high in calories but low in nutrients, just like our pizzas and burgers. In addition, the pet food recalls that made headlines have made some dog owners wary of commercial brands.

High-quality dog food is expensive and even more so if your dog has allergies or specific sensitivities. That's where some DIY skills can come in handy. Believe it or not, cooking homemade dog food is very easy. Most recipes have a small number of ingredients, requiring minimal preparation. The hard part is choosing what should be included in your dog's food rather than cooking it.

This book serves as a comprehensive guide to what makes a healthy and balanced dog diet and how to prepare home meals for your furry companion. Whether you're just looking for homemade treats to make your dog feel special or meal ideas to be in complete control of what your canine companion eats, you came to the right place.

CHAPTER ONE

Why Should You Cook for Your Dog?

There is an unwritten law that dogs should only eat dog food. This notion comes from a good place. Frankly speaking, there are plenty of human foods that a dog should never eat, such as chocolate or avocados, because they are harmful to dogs. So, to avoid unknowingly feeding your dog potentially poisonous food, the simple route is to provide dog food only.

Why should you go through the trouble of cooking food for your dog when they are content with kibble and bone-shaped treats?

High-quality dog food contains all the vitamins and minerals that a dog needs to grow and be healthy. If you only give your dog a certain type of food their entire life, they will most likely eat it without fussing. Dogs are not picky. It's your job to be selective for them. Cooking food for your dog is not about boycotting dog food brands. It's about wanting the best for your canine companion. Even high-quality dog food focuses only on giving your dog a daily intake of nutrients, not on variety or taste. Also, premium as it is, dog food is still a processed product, in and out. It has compounds we are unfamiliar with, which leaves space for doubts and questions. Most dog owners think of their furry companions as their babies. And every good mother wants to know exactly what she is feeding her baby.

With homemade food, you are in full control. You can make sure that all the ingredients are fresh and balanced, to make for a perfectly nutritious meal. You can even make sure that your dog is only eating organic food that has not been chemically treated, as long as you can afford it. Also, cooking for a dog is way easier than cooking for a human. The meal does not have to be fancy or perfect, as long as it contains the right ingredients. Additionally, dog food preparation usually means chopping things up and mixing, boiling, baking, or slow-cooking them. Pretty beginner-friendly and stress-free. Your dog won't judge you; they will just be happy to try something new.

Maybe the biggest reason you should try cooking for your dog is to offer them some variety. Different foods provide different benefits. Like humans, dogs need a balanced intake of animal protein, vegetables, and fibers. When something crucial is missing, you will be able to tell that something is not right. Besides the benefit of variety, cooking for your dog might be a great solution to dealing with allergies and sensitivities. Some dogs have a gluten allergy, and it can be pretty difficult to find the proper food for them. If you cook the food yourself, you can make sure there are no traces of gluten. The result will be a tasty and safe meal for your dog, which will cost you way less than special diet dog kibbles. Some dogs have extremely sensitive intestines, and finding the right food can be a great challenge. By cooking the food, you can avoid anything that would be hard to digest, helping your dog lead a happy, healthy life.

Now, cooking for your dog should not be an "all or nothing" deal. You don't have to commit to cooking every meal for your dog. There are many ways to add variety to your dog's diet. For example, you can add some fresh ingredients to your dog's kibble to give them a nutritional boost. Some good additions to your dog's regular food are a bit of salmon oil, crushed blueberries, or a mixture of chopped vegetables. Similarly, you can choose to keep your dog on their actual food but cook homemade treats for them. These treats will make your dog feel pampered without compromising his health. Homemade treats give some variety to your dog's diet minus the higher risks of obesity that commercial treats come with. And, of course, there is always the possibility to alternate commercial dog food with homemade food. You can give your dog fun weekends or Home-Meal Wednesdays, and they won't complain.

So, why should we cook for our dogs?
- to have control over the ingredients and their quality
- to provide a varied diet for our pooches

- to offer them healthy, nutritious treats
- to create meals that cater to their exact needs
- to pamper our dogs
- because it can be cheaper than buying premium dog food
- because it's easy and stress-free

Those would be the main reasons. We can also argue that going for a raw diet (with uncooked, fresh ingredients) would be closer to what dogs are supposed to eat if they lived in the wild. Dogs can lead a perfectly healthy life on a raw diet. But cooking the ingredients adds a personal touch to things, helps the flavors blend, and makes the food easier to chew and digest.

Dogs are omnivores that need both meat and greens in their diets to be healthy. They also benefit from eating fruits and cereals like rice and oats. So there are plenty of things you can cook for yourself that would also serve as a fitting meal for your dog. Sharing a meal with your dog may serve as a nice bonding experience if you're willing to adjust your tastes to what can be deemed safe for a dog!

The benefits of cooking food for your dog are many. As long as you are aware of what a dog can safely eat and mindful of your dog's particularities, there is no harm in cooking for your dog. In the next chapter, we'll focus on the dos and don'ts of dog nutrition and diets. While the information in this book will give you some solid knowledge of what is beneficial for a dog and what foods to avoid, I strongly recommend talking to a specialist before making any changes in your dog's diet. Before switching their food, you need to consider medical conditions that your dog might have, their breed, age, etc.

Since there is no universal feeding plan to fit all dogs, a vet can help you make the best choices for your dog based on medical history and particularities. Please keep that in mind.

CHAPTER TWO

Dog Nutrition

There is the notion that dogs only need protein, which is not true. Like humans, dogs need essential nutrients—such as protein, fat, carbohydrates, and vitamins—to survive. If you only feed your dog protein, he won't get the essential vitamins he needs, and your dog is bound to have deficiencies that can contribute to thyroid problems. On the other hand, the lack of protein opens him up to other health problems, such as muscle deterioration and blood disorders.

We can't dive into cooking food for dogs if we don't know anything about dog nutrition. Let's take this step by step and focus on the most important aspects of nutrition.

Living organisms need a variety of nutrients to survive and function properly. These are called essential nutrients, and there are six nutrient classes that a dog needs: water, protein, fat, carbohydrates, vitamins, and minerals—pretty much the same essential nutrients that humans need. The difference is that dogs are a bit more particular with the sources and types of these nutrients than humans.

Let's take them one by one and learn how to implement them in our dogs' diets.

Water

Water is the essence of life, and it makes up 60 to 70% of an adult dog's weight. Water has many important functions in the organism, such as aiding digestion, transporting nutrients to cells, regulating body temperature, protecting soft tissues, and getting rid of waste from the body. If there is not enough water in an organism, the repercussions are very severe. A mere 10% decrease in body water can cause serious illnesses, and a 15% decrease can even lead to death.

A dog needs to have a source of fresh, clean water available at all times. It is highly recommended to give your dog tap water that has been thoroughly filtered beforehand. A dog's water requirements vary based on its activity level, environment, diet, and health. For example, if you feed your dog dry food or the outside temperature is high, your dog will drink more water. Usually, a dog instinctively knows how much water it needs, so you just need to make sure that you provide them with enough.

Avoid giving your dog cold or freezing water. Room-temperature water is the way to go. And make sure to refill your dog's water bowl daily with fresh water to prevent it from going stale.

Proteins

Proteins supply energy and amino acids that are essential to life. In an organism, proteins have many roles that make them instrumental to growth and the body's normal functioning. Proteins are one of the main components of hormones, enzymes, antibodies, and neurotransmitters. Thus, we can say that proteins are a vital part of the body's structure, the building blocks of cells, tissues, and organs.

Proteins can't be stored in the body, so the body needs a constant supply of them from food. Also, there are a bunch of essential amino acids that a dog's body can't produce, and they need to get them from their diet. Proteins can be obtained from both animal-based sources and plant-based sources.

Most animal proteins come from lean meats such as chicken, lamb, turkey, beef, rabbit, and fish (especially salmon). Eggs are also excellent sources of proteins because they have a complete amino acid profile. But you should never give your dog raw eggs. Uncooked egg whites contain avidin, which meddles with the metabolism and has harmful effects.

Plant-based sources are vegetables (potatoes, beans, peas, peppers, broccoli, cauliflower) and cereals (rice, oats, corn). However, they are considered incomplete proteins, meaning that they should always be paired up with some animal proteins.

Meat should make up 20% of your dog's food, and it must be lean. Always cut out the fatty parts from the meat you give your dog. Avoid pork meat unless it's 100% lean. Chicken and turkey must always be served cooked and without skin or bones. All meat that does not come from organic farms or trusted sources should be cooked before giving it to your dog.

Puppies and pregnant or lactating females require twice as much protein as a regular dog, so be mindful of that.

Fats

Fats are the top energy suppliers, providing twice the energy of proteins and carbohydrates. Fats are involved in the production of some hormones, allow for fat-soluble vitamins to be absorbed by the organism, allow for the nervous system to develop normally, and form a protective layer around internal organs. This is why they are essential nutrients. From healthy fat sources, a dog gets its share of linoleic acid, omega-3, and omega-6 fatty acids. In the absence of these, the dog does not develop properly and can have skin issues. The body does not produce these essential fatty acids, so they must be included in the food plan.

While dogs need fats in their diets, they have a special sensitivity to fats. A high intake of fats can trigger gastrointestinal issues or pancreatitis. A good idea would be to include fats only in the dog's food and avoid giving your dog fatty food scraps from the table.

The best source of healthy fat you can give your dog is from low-mercury fish and fish oil. Even if you don't commit to cooking food for your dog, a few spoonfuls of fish oil now and then are a great addition to your dog's kibble. Don't go overboard because too much oil can upset a dog's stomach. Plant-based oils like hemp seed or olive oil can also provide healthy fats, as long as you use them in small quantities.

Carbohydrates

Carbohydrates are the main source of glucose in the organism, and glucose is the fuel on which organisms run. However, dogs can make their own glucose if their diet has plenty of proteins and fats. Thus, for dogs, carbohydrates are not essential as a source of energy but as a source of fibers, minerals, vitamins, and antioxidants. Some carbohydrates can alter the state of the bacterial population in the intestine to combat chronic diarrhea. Other moderately fermentable carbohydrates, like beet pulp, rice, and wheat, promote a healthy gut without causing an excess in mucus secretion.

In essence, we can say that carbohydrates promote health in general and provide energy, which allows for proteins and fats to be used for other purposes. However, carbohydrates that have a high content of sugar (potatoes, white bread) should be avoided, as they can lead to a dangerous increase in blood sugar levels. Low-sugar carbs are found in vegetables (beans, peas, carrots, broccoli, zucchini, celery), fruits (banana, blueberries, cantaloupe, watermelon, pears, cored apples), and grains (rice, oats, corn). Healthy low-sugar carbs that are moderately fermentable are great for growing puppies and highly active dogs that burn a lot of energy.

Be aware that some dogs have a gluten allergy. You can make up for it by giving your dog small quantities of boiled potato and corn.

Vitamins

Most vitamins can't be synthesized in the body, which must come from the dog's food. However, only small quantities of vitamins are needed for the organism to function properly. If you provide your dog with a varied, balanced diet, that is enough to give your dog the vitamins they need.

There are two types of vitamins: soluble in fat (A, D, E, K) and soluble in water (B, C). Vitamins have a variety of roles. Vitamin A is known to help the immune system; vitamin D balances out calcium and phosphorus levels; vitamin K allows for the blood to clot when injuries are sustained; vitamins C and E are antioxidants, and vitamin B (especially B12) helps the nervous system develop and work properly.

A useful aspect to keep in mind is that fat-soluble vitamins are stored in the liver and fatty tissue, while the water-soluble ones are not stored in the body. Many owners give vitamin supplements that their dogs don't actually need, leading to hypervitaminosis (an excess of vitamins). The most common and harmful hypervitaminosis are those of vitamin A and D. Excess of vitamin A can cause joint pains, fragile bones, and skin conditions, while an excess of vitamin D can lead to soft tissue calcification (soft tissues become hard, like bones) and kidney issues. Hypervitaminosis does not occur for water-soluble vitamins because the excess is eliminated naturally through urine.

If your dog eats high-quality commercial food, it's most likely that they have the recommended intake of vitamins and does not require supplements.

Vitamin supplements might be needed for a dog that eats home-cooked food, but I strongly recommend seeking a veterinarian's advice before adding any to your dog's meals. You can ensure that your dog gets vitamins by providing a balanced diet with lean meats and dog-friendly vegetables.

Minerals

Minerals, like vitamins, can't be produced by the body, so they need to be provided in the dog's diet. Minerals are involved in many metabolic reactions, they manage fluid balance (sodium, potassium, and chloride), and they are a big part of bone and teeth structure (mostly calcium and phosphorus). Iron has the important role of carrying oxygen molecules through the body to the cells and structures that need it. Zinc is involved in the healing process of wounds, while selenium acts as an antioxidant. Minerals are also crucial to the proper functioning of the nervous system, with magnesium, potassium, calcium, and sodium helping with the transmission of information in the nervous system.

In general, all minerals are required for the body to function normally. But macro minerals (calcium, sodium, potassium, chloride, magnesium, and phosphorus) are needed in higher levels since they are part of many processes. Iron, zinc, selenium, iodine, copper, and manganese are micro minerals. This means they are important but required in lower levels than macro minerals.

Different foods provide different minerals. Meats, for example, are rich in phosphorus, while animal organs like the liver provide iron and copper. Shellfish (lobster, crab, shrimp) contain zinc, and seaweed offers a good intake of magnesium, iodine, and potassium.

Bones are high in calcium, but be mindful of what type of bones you give your dogs. Chicken bones are small, and when they crack, they form tiny shards that can do damage to your dog's insides or cause gastric blockages. Pork bones have the same risks, leading to choking, blockages, and internal damage. The best choice would be raw cow bones, which are the perfect size for your dog to chew on without any worries of choking. However, supervise your dog whenever he's enjoying a bone, just to be on the safe side. Another source of calcium is eggshell. You have to mince the shell until it becomes powdery and mix it in your dog's food. Unfortunately, I can guarantee that your dog will be happier with getting his calcium from cow bones than eggshell powder.

What Is a Balanced Diet for Your Dog?

Your dog's dietary needs change according to the stage of their life. The key to a healthy dog is a well-balanced diet. According to veterinarians, your adult dog's diet should consist of 40–50% carbohydrates, 40% protein, and 10–20% fats. The food you feed your dog must include:

1. carbohydrates for energy,

2. protein,

3. fats, including fatty acids, and

4. vitamins and minerals.

The key to homemade dog food is variety. Rotate the meats and make sure your dog is getting enough vegetables in their diet. Most dogs cannot tolerate a high-fat diet, as it can lead to pancreatitis.

If you are concerned about meeting your dog's nutritional needs, talk to your veterinarian about a multivitamin.

In order to formulate the proper home-cooked diet for your dog, observe what makes them feel more comfortable. Are they happy when they see the meal? Do they happily gulp it down? Be sure to make food for your dog that is healthy and delicious.

Recommended Ingredients

We have already established that your dog's food should be derived from various categories. However, these food categories are composed of many ingredients. Keep in mind that it is important is to prepare your dog's food with fresh ingredients, free from additives.

Protein

When most people think of feeding their dogs protein, beef usually comes to mind. Although dogs do eat beef, there is a variety of protein sources you can give them. Muscles and organs are good sources of protein. However, you should feed your dog liver in moderation because it may retain impurities. Following are sources of protein from which you can choose, depending on their cost and availability:

- turkey, which is easily available and equally easy for dogs to digest;
- ground beef or beef that has been cut into small strips;
- lamb;
- chicken (no bones or skin);
- cow liver;
- chicken liver and hearts;

• fish, although this shouldn't exceed more than two servings a week—salmon and catfish are recommended;
  • eggs should be given in moderation, too; and
  • kidney beans or lima beans, although not as a substitute for meat protein.

Vegetables

There are a variety of vegetables you can feed your dog, including:
  • spinach,
  • cucumbers,
  • carrots,
  • peas,
  • pumpkin,
  • broccoli, although in moderation because it may cause gas,
  • celery,
  • green beans, and
  • cauliflower, although this, too, may cause gas.

Dog-friendly fruits

  • apple (cored),
  • blueberries,
  • pineapple,
  • mango,
  • banana,
  • peach (no pit),
  • cantaloupe, and
  • watermelon (no rind or seeds).

Carbohydrates

Your dog needs carbohydrates that contain fiber that can help maintain healthy digestion. Some carbohydrates you can feed your dog include:
  • oatmeal,
  • rice, particularly brown rice,

• yams,
• cooked potatoes, and
• pasta without oil or salt.

Ingredients You Should Avoid

There is the notion that dogs can eat anything, but this isn't true. Perhaps the most important thing to know is what human foods not to give your dog. Some are toxic to dogs and can even lead to dramatic scenarios such as death if they are frequently ingested by a dog (avocado!). Others are unhealthy because they can lead to obesity, gastrointestinal issues, or other health conditions. Avoid using any of these foods when preparing your dog food:

• **raisins and grapes** are toxic to dogs and may cause severe liver and kidney damage;

• **chocolate**, which can wreak havoc on your dog's metabolic system, causing them to vomit and/or have diarrhea after ingesting even a small amount, while large amounts can lead to heart failure and possibly death;

• **macadamia nuts and walnuts,** which are poisonous for dogs (macadamia nuts, especially) and can affect the nervous system;

• **garlic, onions, leeks, and chives** are toxic for dogs and can cause anemia, making them very weak, quite possibly to the point of collapse (there is a lot of controversy surrounding garlic and whether or not it should be included as an ingredient in dog food, though raw garlic is discouraged);

• **coffee**, which has the same effect on your dog as does chocolate;

• **avocados**, which contain a substance causing dogs to have diarrhea, vomit, and suffer from heart congestion; and

• **yeast** on its own or in dough can cause flatulence and discomfort, and too much gas can cause their stomachs to rupture.

In addition to avoiding the foods mentioned above, don't use spoiled ingredients to make your dog food. One rule that can help guide you for what you should avoid feeding your dog is that anything considered dangerous for you to eat may also be dangerous for your dog.

Ingredients to Use in Moderation

Some ingredients are not harmful to dogs but should still be used in moderation:
- dairy foods, since some dogs may find them hard to digest;
- butter;
- cooking oils, such as canola oil;
- salt, which increases water retention and could lead to heart disease and heart failure; and
- corn, since it is also hard for some dogs to digest.

All mammals have different metabolisms responsible for breaking food down and turning it into energy. This is why certain foods are toxic for dogs but not for humans. It is essential to let the whole family know what your dog can and cannot eat, which will prevent someone from sneaking him a treat that could cause serious health damage.

Above is only a sampling of foods that dogs cannot eat. If you are in doubt about a food item not on the list, check with your veterinarian before feeding it to your dog.

CHAPTER THREE

The Basics of Dog Feeding

The rules for dog feeding vary with the dog's age, breed, and medical conditions. For example, puppies need to be fed multiple times a day, while an adult dog only requires up to two meals a day. Similarly, a golden retriever will need a considerably larger amount of food than a chihuahua, and an obese dog will need to follow a strict diet in order to become healthy. So, strictly speaking, every dog needs a personalized feeding schedule based on age, breed, activity level, medical conditions, and sensibilities. Usually, you can tell if your dog is eating enough if he keeps his figure and is energetic rather than passive. A specialist can help you determine what, when, and how much you should feed your dog, and I highly recommend you seek advice from your local veterinarian!

Keeping all this in mind, let's go through some general rules to give you a better understanding of dog nutrition.

Puppies

Puppies are undergoing a constant growth process, so they need a lot of energy. However, be careful not to accelerate the puppy's growth rate by giving them a lot of food. Puppies are prone to overeating if given a chance, which can lead to future health problems, especially for medium and large dog breeds. If they gain weight too fast, these larger breeds can suffer from bone or joint issues that render them unable to walk properly.

It is recommended that puppies have several small meals a day until they are potty-trained. After that, it is recommended they be fed three to four times a day until they are nine months old, as their metabolic system is working overtime, and they will need more calories.

If you want to train your dog, scheduling meal times is a big part of making sure that your puppy will grow to be an obedient and well-behaved adult. Small breeds usually reach their adult body weight in about nine to twelve months, while a larger breed will keep growing until fifteen months.

Make sure your dog has access to fresh water all day, every day.

Adults

An adult pet should be fed based on their size and activity levels. A dog that is a notorious couch potato does not consume the same amount of energy as a dog that accompanies you on your daily jogs or a dog that takes part in dog agility competitions.

A dog with an average activity level, meaning that they are not a complete lap dog but not a daily exercise type, requires a "maintenance" level of energy. Your dog's "maintenance" amounts vary with their size and environmental conditions (like temperature). A veterinarian can help you determine your dog's maintenance level. Our couch potato can require as little as 10% of their breed's maintenance energy, while a very active dog will most likely need more than their breed's average energy. A police dog or a cattle dog with a high workload and considerable stress level might need an extra 50 to 70% of their breed's maintenance energy.

A good rule of thumb is to give your adult dog two meals a day. Divide their daily necessities of food into two meals, one in the morning and one in the evening.

But there are many ways to go about feeding your dog. You can provide a bowl of food that is always available to your dog, allowing them to eat how much they want when they want. This is called free-choice feeding, and it is recommended for nursing mothers and dogs that don't tend to overeat. There is also time-feeding, which involves leaving a portion of food out for your dog for a specific period of time (say 30 or 40 minutes). When the time is up, the food that has not been consumed is removed. The last and most common feeding practice is portion-control feeding. You carefully measure the amount of food you give your dog daily to prevent overeating and obesity.

Take into consideration that a sick dog or a dog recovering from surgery might need more food than usual to help them heal and fight the disease. Ask your vet whether your dog's nutritional needs have changed if your dog has undergone surgery or is battling a chronic disease.

Another thing to consider regarding nutrition is how many treats you give your dog. Treats should only make up 5% or less of the dog's food intake to prevent health conditions such as obesity. Use treats as special rewards or motivation, and go for small treats. We'll provide in this book some great healthy home-cooked treat ideas to pamper your dog and motivate them to be on their best behavior.

How much?

How active your dog is and his age will determine how much he should eat daily. Here's a basic guideline to consider.

DOGS WEIGHT	AMOUNT PER DAY
3 pounds	⅓ cup to ½ cup
5 pounds	½ cup to ⅔ cup
10 pounds	¾ cup to 1 cup
20 pounds	1 cup to 1½ cups
40 pounds	2¼ cups to 3 cups
80 pounds	3 to 4 cups

The above chart is a basic guideline recommending how much your dog should eat in 24 hours. Most adult dogs eat twice a day, so you will need to divide the amount in half to make two meals.

Use a measuring cup to measure your dog's daily portions. If you are freezing homemade food, pre-measure everything to the proper meal size. This will save you some time later.

Senior dogs

Since smaller dog breeds live longer than larger breeds, they show age-related changes at a later age. You can accurately decide if your dog can be considered a senior based on a dog's size. Small dogs fit the senior mark at about 10–12 years old; medium-sized dogs enter their old age at about 8–9 years old; large dog breeds become seniors at the age of 6–7 years old, and giant dog breeds can be considered seniors at the age of 5. A senior diet focuses on maintaining the dog's health while managing chronic conditions and body weight.

Some commercial "senior diet" foods have a low level of protein. Try to avoid those, as studies have shown that protein requirements for a dog do not decrease with age. Older dogs need a good amount of protein to help maintain their muscle mass. However, you should focus on a low-calorie diet, as senior dogs tend to put on body fat due to changes in the metabolic rate or the decrease in activity levels that come with old age. Also, a senior diet should include healthy fatty acids to help them keep their coats and skin healthy and moderately fermentable carbohydrates to promote the growth of beneficial intestinal bacteria to prevent gastrointestinal issues. Similarly, antioxidants like vitamins E and C are very beneficial for older dogs, as they boost immunity and help the organism deal with the signs of aging.

When taking care of a senior dog, you should plan for a daily feeding routine to not stress out the animal. If you want to add something to their diet or change their food in any way, make sure to introduce them to the new things gradually to avoid gastrointestinal issues.

Try to have your dog medically examined as often as possible to allow your vet to track chronic diseases and offer you advice regarding your senior's diet.

CHAPTER FOUR

Tips for Making Homemade Dog Food

Deciding to give your dog homemade food can be one of the best decisions you will ever make. Homemade dog food is healthy, economical, and can be easily made. Following are some useful tips.

Take Time to Prepare Your Dog Food

Find the time to make the food. Just as when cooking for your family, use good, safe food handling practices, especially when using raw meats. Give yourself time to pack the cooked food in freezer bags, measured in portions appropriate for your dog.

Buy High-Quality Ingredients in Bulk

Buying ingredients in bulk will lower the cost, saving you money. Choose good, high-quality meats and organic chicken whenever possible. You can prepare the homemade dog food in larger batches and freeze them in daily portion sizes.

Dietary Supplements

Many dog owners who choose to make home-cooked meals for their dogs also give them dietary supplements (like fish oil), taking the dog's size into consideration.

If your dog is only eating home-cooked meals, try to balance variety with consistency. You want your dog to get essential nutrients, but you don't want to overwhelm their digestive systems. Settle on two types of meat that your dog favors and switch the vegetables around while also providing nutritious fruity treats or dietary supplements. Find two or three recipes that your dog likes and work with them!

Portion Control

An important point to remember is portion control. Even though homemade dog food is wholesome and healthy, too much of it can cause weight gain, leading to health issues for your dog.

Switch Gradually

Although your dog's health will improve when you serve them homemade meals, you should be patient because it will take them some time to adjust to their new meals. Changing your dog's food too fast can cause them to have diarrhea or an upset tummy. Switch their diet by mixing the new, homemade food with the old, commercial dog food at first, slowly weaning out the processed food.

Always ask for a specialist's advice before adding something to your dog's diet or changing your dog's diet. If possible, check food recipes with your vet to make sure that the food would be beneficial for your dog and to help you decide on appropriate serving sizes.

Avoid Refreezing Dog Food

If you put leftovers in the freezer, try to serve them for a maximum of 3 months. You can store leftovers in zipper bags or plastic containers. If you cook daily for your dog, it's a good idea to label each bag/container with the date you made it before putting it in the freezer.

Avoid refreezing dog food. Never serve your dog cold/freezing food. Allow the food to defrost overnight in the refrigerator.

CHAPTER FIVE

Recipes for Homemade Dog Meals

Although preparing your dog's food will take time, the results will be worth it. The recipes in this chapter will make it easier for you to prepare homemade meals for your dog. Watch your dog to make sure they don't have an allergy or adverse reaction to any of the meals. Once you know what your dog likes, you'll know exactly how to provide them with healthy and delicious food.

Crockpot Beef with Vegetables

Yield: 10 cups
Ingredients:
1 pound lean ground beef
½ cup carrots, sliced
1 can red kidney beans (15-ounce), drained and rinsed
½ cup whole-grain rice
½ cup frozen peas
½ cup butternut squash, sliced

Directions:
1. Mix all ingredients into a large slow cooker (6-qt), stir them vigorously, and add 4 cups of water.

2. Cover the mixture and cook it either on low heat for 5 to 6 hours or on high heat for 2 to 3 hours. Stir from time to time to make sure that everything is nicely cooked.

3. Let the meal cool off before serving.

4. You can put leftovers in the freezer and save them for another time.

Nutritional Information (Per 1 Cup Serving)

Calories: 138; Fat: 3.1 g; Carbohydrates: 10.4 g; Protein: 16.7 g

This recipe is beginner-friendly, as you only have to chop the ingredients and put them in a slow cooker. You can add other vegetables like broccoli, cauliflower, and bell peppers or try it with different meat, such as turkey, lamb, or salmon.

Don't be afraid to play with this recipe! If you give your dog variety, you make sure that their diet is balanced, and you allow them to develop their taste for the finer things. Soon enough, they will have favorite foods, and they will let you know what they prefer.

Beef Stew

Yield: 4 cups
Ingredients:
1 small sweet potato
1 pound stewing beef
½ cup carrots, diced
½ cup green beans, diced
1 cup water

Directions:
1. Put the sweet potato in the microwave and cook for 5–8 minutes, until tender but firm.
2. Dice the sweet potato.
3. Slice stewing beef into nickel-sized chunks. Sauté the beef in a pot for 4–5 minutes over medium heat.
4. Gradually add the water, carrots, green beans, and sweet potato.
5. Bring to a boil. Reduce heat and simmer for about 15 minutes to allow carrots to become tender.
6. Let cool and serve.

Nutritional Information (Per 1 Cup Serving)
Calories: 234; Fat: 7.1 g; Carbohydrates: 5.4 g; Protein: 35.1 g

This recipe is a version of human beef stew, but some adjustments have been made to make it suitable for dogs. It consists of vegetables for vitamins and meat for protein. This recipe is a good substitute for wet, commercial dog foods. You can store the extra stew in your fridge and serve it to your dog later.

Stir Fry Meal

Yield: 6 cups
Ingredients:
1 pound lean ground beef
2 ounces whole-wheat pasta
1 cup broccoli, chopped
5 medium carrots, chopped
2 cups water

Directions:
1. Add beef, broccoli, carrots, and water to a saucepan. Bring to a boil.
2. Add pasta. Let simmer for about twenty minutes.
3. Cool before serving.

Nutritional Information (Per 1 Cup Serving)
Calories: 236; Fat: 5.1 g; Carbohydrates: 19.7 g; Protein: 26.8 g

This easy stir fry is great for your dog, and it doesn't require too many ingredients.

Doggy Omelet with Salmon and Spinach

Yield: 2 cups

Ingredients:

3 ounces salmon, deboned and skinned

½ cup spinach, chopped

1 teaspoon olive oil

2 eggs

Directions:

1. Put the olive oil in a non-stick skillet, and heat it over medium heat.

2. Add the salmon, add the spinach and let it heat, making sure the fish is cooked.

3. Crack the eggs and stir your ingredients for about 2 minutes or until you're sure there is no raw egg left.

4. Let it cool down properly and serve it to your hungry pooch.

Nutritional Information (Per 1 Cup Serving)

Calories: 141; Fat: 9.4 g; Carbohydrates: 0.6 g; Protein: 14 g

This recipe is better served fresh, so I'd recommend not keeping leftovers in the freezer. Be mindful of the amount of oil you use, as too much can have a nasty effect on your dog's digestive system. Instead of spinach, you can use broccoli to mix this up a bit.

Be sure to check in with your vet if this recipe would be suitable for your dog.

Turkey and Vegetables Delight

Yield: 8 cups

Ingredients:

3 pounds ground turkey

½ cup whole-grain rice

1 tablespoon vegetable oil

½ cup frozen peas

3 cups baby spinach, chopped

2 carrots, shredded

1 zucchini, shredded

Directions:

1. Cook the rice according to package instructions and set it aside.

2. Heat the oil in a stockpot or a thick-walled cooking pot over medium heat.

3. Add the turkey and let it cook for 3 to 5 minutes until it turns brown. Don't forget to stir it so it's evenly cooked.

4. Add the rice and the vegetables, and keep the mixture on heat for another 3 to 5 minutes. Stir energetically until all the ingredients are properly cooked.

5. Let the meal cool off before serving.

6. You can divide the leftovers into servings and put them in the freezer for another time.

Nutritional Information (Per 1 Cup Serving)

Calories: 298; Fat: 15.9 g; Carbohydrates: 6 g; Protein: 31.3 g

You can play around with this recipe by adding (be aware you'll end up with more food, so stick to adding one or two new elements) or replacing vegetables. You can replace spinach with broccoli and peas with green beans or choose for yourself what vegetables to treat your dog with. Just make sure they are all dog-friendly. If you want to try the recipe without rice, you can use cauliflower or quinoa.

You can also replace the meat with beef, lamb, or chicken and add a crumbled hardboiled egg for some more animal protein. Try not to have two different types of meat (for example, beef and chicken). Stick with one at a time.

Doggie Meatballs

Yield: 30 meatballs
Ingredients:
4 pounds ground beef
1 cup oat bran
1½ cups pumpkin puree
2 large carrots, boiled and mashed
1 slice bread, broken into small pieces
2 eggs, beaten
Olive oil for cookie sheets

Directions:
1. Preheat oven to 350° F (177°C).
2. Put all ingredients in a large bowl. Mix everything by hand and form it into meatballs the size of a doughnut hole.
3. Place on cookie sheets greased with olive oil, spaced evenly, taking care not to place too closely together.
4. Bake in the oven for about 25 minutes or until thoroughly cooked.
5. Let cool. Divide into Ziploc bags according to daily portion needs.

Nutritional Information (Per 1 Meatball)
Calories: 177; Fat: 10.4 g; Carbohydrates: 3.9 g; Protein: 16.9 g

This is a wonderful option for older dogs who might have a hard time eating, as the meatballs will be easy to pick up and eat. The pumpkin is a natural stool softener, ideal for your older dog.

Pork & Eggs

Yield: 6 cups

Ingredients:

2 slices white bread

¼ pound ground pork

2 eggs, hardboiled

2 cups white rice

Directions:

1. Make sure eggs are cooked properly before chopping them.

2. Cook ground pork in a non-stick skillet over medium heat, draining away any excess fat.

3. Mix the pork with eggs.

4. Cook rice like you usually would.

5. Chop bread, removing the crust.

6. Add bread to egg and pork mixture.

7. Combine all ingredients and serve. Make sure you refrigerate any leftovers.

Nutritional Information (Per 1 Cup Serving)

Calories: 281; Fat: 2.6 g; Carbohydrates: 50.9 g; Protein: 11.4 g

You'll find this recipe is full of protein, lacking anything that will raise your dog's bad cholesterol.

Chicken and Vegetable Medley

Yield: 6 cups

Ingredients:

1 pound boneless, skinned chicken breasts, cubed

2 cups vegetable medley, frozen

2 cups brown rice, cooked

Directions:

1. Heat a large skillet over medium heat. Add chicken and cook for 5 minutes.

2. Add vegetable medley and brown rice. Cook for 5–10 minutes, mixing thoroughly.

3. Remove from heat. Let cool completely before serving.

4. Refrigerate any leftovers.

Nutritional Information (Per 1 Cup Serving)

Calories: 155; Fat: 2.3 g; Carbohydrates: 14.6 g; Protein: 17.7 g

Dogs love chicken as much as beef, and your dog will love this low-fat meal.

Chicken Casserole

Yield: 7 cups

Ingredients:

2 pounds boneless, skinned chicken breasts

½ cup carrots, chopped

½ cup rolled oats

½ cup green beans, chopped

4 cups chicken broth, no salt added

½ cup broccoli, chopped

Directions:

1. Remove excess fat from chicken breasts before cutting them into small chunks the size of nickels.

2. Heat non-stick skillet over medium heat and cook chicken breasts until no longer pink.

3. Put vegetables, chicken broth, and chicken inside a large pot. Bring to boil and simmer for about 15 minutes or until you notice the carrots have become tender.

4. Let cool before serving.

Nutritional Information (Per 1 Cup Serving)
Calories: 200; Fat: 4.4 g; Carbohydrates: 6.2 g; Protein: 31.4 g

The leftover portion can last up to five days in the fridge. If the chicken breasts stick to the skillet, try frying in a small amount of olive oil.

Chicken provides your dog with a good amount of protein, and the vegetables help give the meal additional flavor. This meal is recommended for your dog because the vegetables will help your dog have a healthy intestinal tract, while the green beans are important for making your dog feel full.

Easy Chicken Stew

Yield: 6 cups

Ingredients:

1 pound chicken chunks

2 celery sticks

2 medium carrots

1 cup brown rice

2 cups water

Directions:

1. Chop vegetables.

2. Place chicken chunks in a pot with chopped celery and carrots.

3. Add brown rice and water. Bring to boil. Reduce heat to low. Cover and cook for 30 minutes until brown rice is done.

4. Serve once cooled. Place any leftovers in the fridge.

Nutritional Information (Per 1 Cup Serving)
Calories: 210; Fat: 2.7 g; Carbohydrates: 26.5 g; Protein: 18.5 g

This is another easy recipe that will provide all of the nutrition your dog needs.

Doggie Chili

Yield: 10 cups

Ingredients:

2 pounds boneless, skinned chicken breasts

1 cup carrots, diced

4 cups chicken broth, no salt added

1 cup kidney beans, drained

½ cup tomato paste

1 cup black beans, drained

Directions:

1. Remove excess fat from chicken breasts and dice into nickel-sized pieces.

2. Use a non-stick skillet to cook chicken breasts, removing them when no longer pink.

3. Combine carrots, chicken broth, beans, chicken, and tomato paste in a large pot and heat over medium heat. Let cook for about 10 minutes.

4. Let mixture cool and serve.

Nutritional Information (Per 1 Cup Serving)
Calories: 262; Fat: 3.4 g; Carbohydrates: 27.3 g; Protein: 30.2 g

The leftover chili can feed your dog for up to five days. You can also add ½ tablespoon fish oil to the chili, resulting in good, strong flavors that your dog will love.

For dogs to stay healthy and active, they require huge quantities of protein, which they can get from whole meat sources, especially where puppies are concerned. A good example of protein is fresh chicken. Beans can also provide a significant amount of protein.

Gourmet Chicken Cake for Dogs

Yield: 8 cups

Ingredients:

2½ pounds boneless, skinned chicken breasts

1 cup brown rice

1 medium-sized apple, cored, peeled, and chopped

½ cup carrots, chopped

½ cup corn, unsweetened

½ cup peas

1 egg, with shell

Directions:

1. Prepare your oven by preheating it at 325°F (163°C).

2. Cook the corn, peas, and carrots in a pot to tender.

3. Mush the vegetable mixture together in a bowl, creating a veggie paste.

4. Cook the rice according to the packaging, then add it over the veggie paste.

5. Slice your chicken in tiny strips or mince it with a food processor. Make sure that you discard any fatty tissue you find.

6. Crack the egg in a bowl and crush the shell until it becomes a powdery substance.

7. Put the egg, chicken, and apple together in a mixing bowl.

8. Prepare a cake pan by lining it with baking paper.

9. Take half of the chicken-apple-egg mixture and place it at the bottom of your cake pan. Place a layer of rice-veggie mix (about ⅔ of the whole mixture) over it.

10. Add the remaining chicken mixture and top it off with a final layer of rice-veggie mix. Now you created your layered cake!

11. Put your cake into the oven and let it cook for about 35 minutes, or until the juices are clear. You can cut a piece of cake and inspect it to make sure there is no pinkish meat.

12. When it's done, cut an appropriately-sized slice for your dog and let it cool before serving it.

13. The leftovers can be stored in the fridge for up to five days.

Nutritional Information (Per 1 Cup Serving)
Calories: 282; Fat: 4.4 g; Carbohydrates: 25.8 g; Protein: 33.2 g

This recipe is a bit more complex because it involves many steps. But, if you take it one step at a time, it's pretty straightforward. Just chop, mix and layer your ingredients!

If you want to mix up this recipe, you can replace chicken with turkey, and instead of carrots, you can try adding pumpkin. The taste will be similar enough, and plenty of dogs prefer turkey over chicken.

Make sure here that the eggshell is pulverized so there won't be any sharp bits left for your dog to bite into. Also, be careful with the meat. It's better to cut a bit into the cake and make sure there's no pink on sight, just to make sure. After all, it's a meal for your dog; they won't mind if it doesn't look perfect.

Liver Dinner

Yield: 4 cups
Ingredients:
1 cup corn
1 tablespoon olive oil
1 pound chicken liver
2 cups green beans, trimmed
2 tablespoons all-purpose flour

Directions:
1. Cut chicken liver into strips and mix with flour.
2. In a non-stick skillet, heat olive oil over medium heat. Add chicken liver. Cook for 2 minutes.
3. Add corn and green beans. Cover and cook for 7–10 minutes, until green beans are cooked through.
4. Don't be alarmed by the color! Your dog will love this dish.
5. Serve cooled and refrigerate leftovers, but serve warm.

Nutritional Information (Per 1 Cup Serving)
Calories: 225; Fat: 9.5 g; Carbohydrates: 15 g; Protein: 21.7 g

Most dogs love liver, making this a healthy and delicious meal for your pet.

Turkey Dinner with Carrots and Green Beans

Yield: 10 cups
Ingredients:
1 pound ground turkey
4 cups water
1 cup carrots, chopped
2 cups brown rice
1 cup green beans, chopped

Directions:
1. Heat non-stick skillet over medium heat. Add ground turkey. Cook until the turkey is no longer pink. Set aside.

2. Heat a large pot over medium-high heat. Add turkey, brown rice, and water, and bring to a boil.

3. Dial the heat down to medium and let the mixture cook for another 15 minutes or until you notice the rice has become soft and tender.

4. Add green beans and carrots to the mixture and cook for 5–10 minutes until the vegetables are tender.

5. Let cool and serve to your dog.

Nutritional Information (Per 1 Cup Serving)
Calories: 225; Fat: 6.1 g; Carbohydrates: 30.8 g; Protein: 11.1 g

Leftovers can be stored in the fridge for 3–5 days. When preparing this recipe, avoid using heavy oils because they have a high-fat content that may upset your dog's stomach.

Turkey gives your dog protein, while vegetables contain minerals and additional vitamins. This recipe is especially suitable for puppies in need of shedding some pounds since it has less fat when compared to dishes made with beef.

Pumpkin Beef Stew

Yield: 4 cups

Ingredients:

1 pound lean beef stew meat

1 small potato

½ cup pumpkin, chopped

½ cup frozen peas, thawed

¼ cup whole-grain flour

½ cup water

Directions:

1. Boil the potato or put it in the microwave for a few minutes until it becomes tender and set it aside.

2. Slice your beef into small bits and cook it in a non-stick skillet for 10 to 15 minutes over medium heat. You want it to be well-done.

3. Set the beef aside but don't throw away the drippings.

4. Heat the remaining drippings over medium-low heat and slowly add the flour and the water. Use a whisk to mix these ingredients and create a thick concoction.

5. Slice the potato and add it to the mix alongside the carrots, peas, pumpkin, and cooked beef.

6. Let it cook for about 10 minutes or until the carrots become tender. Don't forget to stir so the stew can cook evenly.

7. Wait for the stew to cool off and serve the recommended amount to your eager pup.

8. You can keep the leftovers in the fridge for up to 5 days or freeze them to keep them fresh.

Nutritional Information (Per 1 Cup Serving)

Calories: 244; Fat: 6.3 g; Carbohydrates: 18.2 g; Protein: 28.3 g

Instead of pumpkin, you can use carrots or baby carrots, and you can replace peas with chopped green beans. The nice thing about dog food recipes is that you can mix and match and see whatever version your dog enjoys most. If your dog has a gluten allergy, replace the whole-grain flour with brown rice flour or almond flour.

Doggy Meatloaf

Yield: 5 cups
Ingredients:
½ pound ground pork
½ pound ground beef
½ cup ricotta cheese
1 egg, beaten
1 cup rolled oats
1 cup vegetable medley, frozen

Directions:
1. Preheat oven to 375°F. Grease a meatloaf pan.
2. In a large bowl, mix ingredients together.
3. Press mixture into pan. Bake for 40–50 minutes.
4. Slice and serve once cooled. Refrigerate leftovers.

Nutritional Information (Per 1 Cup Serving)
Calories: 341; Fat: 21.5 g; Carbohydrates: 14 g; Protein: 21.5 g

Fruit Parfait

Yield: 2 cups
Ingredients:
½ cup nonfat yogurt
½ cup applesauce
½ cup strawberries, diced
½ cup blueberries, diced

Directions:
1. Mix all ingredients in a medium-sized bowl. Make sure fruit is well-blended and yogurt is smooth.
2. Serve to your dog in small amounts.

Nutritional Information (Per 1 Cup Serving)
Calories: 94; Fat: 0.3 g; Carbohydrates: 21.9 g; Protein: 2.4 g

It's good to treat your dog to dessert now and then. Your puppy will enjoy the great taste of this fruit parfait and benefit from its protein and vitamins.

This fruit parfait can be stored in the fridge for 3–5 days. This mixture is quite heavy, so it's advisable to reduce the quantity of regular food you give your dog when you feed them the fruit parfait.

Quinoa Dish

Yield: 10 cups
Ingredients:
4 cups water
2 cups quinoa
2 large sweet potatoes
2 cups sweet peas

Directions:
1. In a saucepan, add water and quinoa, and bring to a boil. Reduce heat, cover, and simmer for 15–20 minutes until quinoa is tender. Once done, set aside.
2. Peel sweet potatoes and microwave for 10 minutes. Dice potatoes.
3. Heat a non-stick skillet over medium heat. Add potatoes and sweet peas. Cook for about 10 minutes.
4. Let quinoa cool and combine with the sweet potatoes.
5. Serve warm. Store leftovers in the fridge.

Nutritional Information (Per 1 Cup Serving)
Calories: 175; Fat: 2.2 g; Carbohydrates: 32.6 g; Protein: 6.8 g

This meal is filling and good for your dog's diet once done smartly. Quinoa is a great way to introduce your pet to healthy grains.

CHAPTER SIX

Recipes for Dog Treats

What better way to reward your dog than to prepare delicious treats for them? Here are some recipes you can try.

Heart-Shaped Chicken Treats

Yield: 12 treats

Ingredients:

1 silicon hearts mold (make sure that it can be put in the oven) – This recipe is enough to fill a mold with 12 small hearts (ice cube-sized).

½ cup brown rice, cooked

1 cup boneless chicken breast, finely sliced

1 egg, beaten

3 tablespoons whole-grain flour

Directions:

1. Prepare the oven by preheating it to 350°F.

2. Blend all the ingredients in a food processor or a blender. You can also mix them by hand.

3. Using a spoon, put the mixture into the silicone molds.

4. Bake your chicken hearts for 20–30 minutes until the tops of the hearts turn brown.

5. Let them cool down before removing them from the molds and serving them to your dog.

6. They can be stored in the fridge for about 5 days, and they can last in the freezer for up to 3 weeks.

Nutritional Information (Per Treat)

Calories: 54; Fat: 0.9 g; Carbohydrates: 7.5 g; Protein: 3.8 g

If you want to be sure that the egg is cooked properly, you can boil it for a few minutes before mashing it and adding it to the mix.

Feel free to use any heat-resistant mold, just make sure to go for one with 12 little shapes.

Basic Dog Biscuits

Yield: 12 dog biscuits

Ingredients:

1 egg, beaten

2 cups whole-wheat flour (great for dogs sensitive to oats or white flour)

½ cup hot water

1 teaspoon chicken bouillon powder

You can add other optional ingredients, including liver powder, shredded cheese, eggs, chicken, or bacon.

Directions:

1. Preheat oven to 350°F.

2. Put bouillon in hot water to dissolve. Add the rest of the ingredients.

3. Knead the dough for about 3 minutes to form a ball.

4. Roll the dough to a thickness of ½ inch. Cut it with a bone-shaped cookie cutter.

5. Lightly grease a cookie sheet and place cookies on it.

6. Bake for about 30 minutes.

Nutritional Information (Per Biscuit)

Calories: 81; Fat: 0.6 g; Carbohydrates: 15.9 g; Protein: 2.6 g

You can customize these biscuits to your dog's taste.

Bacon Peanut Butter Biscuits

Yield: 18 biscuits

Ingredients:

1 cup creamy peanut butter, no salt added

¾ cup milk

1 egg, beaten

2 cups whole-wheat flour

⅓ cup rolled oats

3 strips cooked bacon, chopped

Directions:

1. Preheat oven to 325°F. Lightly grease a cookie sheet.

2. Combine peanut butter, milk, oats, bacon, and egg in a bowl. Add flour and mix until combined into a thick dough. Knead slightly on a countertop to thoroughly combine ingredients if needed.

3. Using a rolling pin, roll your dough until it reaches a thickness of about ¼ inch on a well-floured surface. Cut with a bone-shaped cookie cutter. Arrange evenly on the cookie sheet.

4. Bake for 18–20 minutes. Take the cookie sheet out of the oven and flip cookies using a spatula.

5. Bake for 10 more minutes or until lightly browned.

6. Let cool completely before giving it to your pup as a treat.

7. Store at room temperature for 1 week or freeze.

Nutritional Information (Per Biscuit)

Calories: 156; Fat: 8.5 g; Carbohydrates: 15 g; Protein: 6.3 g

Bacon and peanut butter are every dog's favorite snacks. Your dog will be begging for more of these biscuits.

Veggie Dog Treats

Yield: about 20 treats, depending on the chosen cutter
Ingredients:
1 carrot, peeled and shredded
1 zucchini, shredded
1 cup fresh baby spinach, chopped
1 cup pumpkin puree
¼ cup pumpkin seed butter
½ cup of oats
3 cups whole-grain flour
2 eggs, beaten
cookie cutters of preferred shapes

Directions:
1. Prepare your oven by preheating it to 350°F. Line a baking sheet with baking paper and leave it close by.

2. In a mixer bowl, add the pumpkin puree, eggs, and pumpkin seed butter. Using the paddle attachment of an electric mixer, beat the ingredients on medium-high speed for about 2 minutes.

3. Lower the speed and gradually add the oats and flour until your dough no longer sticks to everything. Then you can add the veggies and let them mix until they are thoroughly incorporated into the mixture.

4. Scatter a bit of flour on a surface and knead your dough until it comes together.

5. Using a rolling pin, roll your dough until it reaches a thickness of about ¼ inch.

6. Now the fun part. Get your cookie cutters, cut out the doggie treats, and put them on the baking sheet.

7. Bake for about 20–25 minutes until the edges of the treats turn golden brown.

8. Let them cool before serving them to your dog.

9. The treats can be stored in the fridge for a few days.

If your dough is still sticky after kneading, add some oat flour.

The consistency of these treats is more on the chewy side rather than crunchy.

You can use gluten-free flour if your dog has a gluten allergy.

Nutritional Information (Per Treat)
Calories: 114; Fat: 3.6 g; Carbohydrates: 17 g; Protein: 5.6 g

Gingerbread Treats

Yield: 10–20 treats
Ingredients:
6 ounces whole-grain flour
3 ounces peanut butter
4 tablespoons hot water
½ teaspoon ground cinnamon
2 teaspoons ground ginger

Directions:
1. Preheat oven to 350°F.
2. Mix peanut butter and hot water in a bowl, stirring well.
3. Add cinnamon, ginger, and flour, mix until it forms a dough. You may need to add a little more water if necessary.
4. Knead the dough with hands before flattening to ¼ inch thickness. Slice as desired.
5. Bake for 15–20 minutes and let cool before serving.

Nutritional Information Per Treat (1 of 10 total)
Calories: 113; Fat: 4.5 g; Carbohydrates: 15 g; Protein: 3.9 g

Ginger is another great way to add flavor to your dog treats, making this the perfect recipe.

Mint Treats

Yield: 10–20 treats

Ingredients:

3 tablespoons mint, chopped

2 cups whole-grain flour

1 egg, beaten

1 tablespoon raw honey

Directions:

1. Preheat oven to 350°F.

2. Mix the mint, flour, egg, and honey in a large bowl. Combine to form a dough. You may need to add a little water.

3. Roll your dough until it reaches a thickness of about ¼ inch.

4. Get your cookie cutters, cut out the doggie treats, and put them on a greased baking sheet.

5. Bake for about 30 minutes

6. Let cool before serving.

Nutritional Information Per Treat (1 of 10 total)

Calories: 95; Fat: 0.9 g; Carbohydrates: 19.3 g; Protein: 3.9 g

This is a crunchy treat flavored with mint that is great for your dog's teeth and digestive system.

Treats for Diabetic Dogs

Yield: 10 treats

Ingredients:

½ pound beef liver, finely sliced

½ cup whole-grain flour

2 eggs, beaten

Directions:

1. Prepare your oven by preheating it to 350°F. Line a jelly roll pan (10x15 inch) with parchment paper.

2. Use a food processor to cut the beef liver into tiny pieces.

3. Put the beef liver, flour, and eggs in a bowl, and stir them with a wooden spoon.

4. Spread the mixture onto the jelly roll pan. Try to level it as best as you can.

5. Bake your mixture for up to 15 minutes, making sure that the center is firm.

6. Wait for the food to cool off. Then use cookie cutters to cut individual treats.

7. Serve the treats to your hungry pup!

8. Store the leftovers in the fridge in a sealed container for up to 4 days.

Nutritional Information (Per Treat)

Calories: 63; Fat: 1.8 g; Carbohydrates: 5.2 g; Protein: 6.5 g

You can play around with this recipe by replacing the liver with turkey or chicken or using beef kidneys.

Almond and Banana Treats

Yield: 10 treats

Ingredients:

1 teaspoon ground cinnamon

½ banana, mashed

¾ cup almond butter, unsalted

1 egg, beaten

Directions:

1. Preheat oven to 350°F. Line a baking sheet with parchment paper.

2. Mash banana in a bowl and add the rest of the ingredients.

3. Blend together and spoon onto the parchment paper.

4. Bake for 10 minutes.

5. Let cool before serving.

Nutritional Information (Per Treat)

Calories: 131; Fat: 11.5 g; Carbohydrates: 5.6 g; Protein: 3.5 g

Dogs love almonds almost as much as peanut butter, making this a great treat.

Homemade Chicken Jerky

Yield: 10–20 chicken strips
Ingredients:
2 pounds chicken breasts, boneless and skinless

Directions:
1. Prepare your oven by preheating it to 200°F.
2. Trim the chicken breasts by removing any fatty tissue.
3. Cut your chicken into strips (about ⅛ inch thick) using a paring knife.
4. Put them on a greased baking sheet and bake them for 2 to 3 hours. You'll know they are cooked when you can snap small pieces off.
5. Let the strips cool down before serving them to your dog.
6. You can store them in the fridge (in airtight containers or zip bags) for up to 2 weeks.

Nutritional Information Per Strip (1 of 10 total)
Calories: 103; Fat: 2.3 g; Carbohydrates: 0 g; Protein: 19.2 g

With this recipe, you can also make beef strips, turkey strips, and venison strips.

Vegetable Jerky

Yield: 30–40 strips
Ingredients:
2 medium sweet potatoes
1 large banana
1 cup applesauce
1½ cups carrots, sliced
2 cups oats
3 cups whole-wheat flour
½ cup water

Directions:
1. Preheat oven to 360°F.
2. Peel sweet potatoes. Microwave for 10 minutes. Dice.
3. In a large bowl, mash the banana and add sweet potatoes.
4. Add oats, flour, and carrots.
5. Add water and applesauce. Mix until a dough forms.
6. Roll the dough to a thickness of ½ inch and cut into strips.
7. Place on a greased baking sheet and bake for 30 minutes.
8. Store jerky in the fridge for 2–3 weeks.

Nutritional Information Per Strip (1 of 30 total)
Calories: 96; Fat: 0.5 g; Carbohydrates: 20.8 g; Protein: 2.4 g

This vegetable jerky is the perfect source of vitamin A, protein, carbs, and potassium.

Sweet Potato Chews

Yield: 20–30 treats
Ingredient:
2 sweet potatoes

Directions:
1. Wash sweet potatoes thoroughly before peeling them.
2. Slice into ¼ inch slices (you can do this by cutting down the middle, which should act as their length).
3. Set dehydrator to 145–155°F, which is usually the highest, and leave at that temperature until slices are completely dried. This will take about 6–8 hours to give the slices a chewy texture. If you want the treat to be crunchier, extend the dehydration period until you achieve the texture you desire.

Nutritional Information Per Treat (1 of 20 total)
Calories: 15; Fat: 0 g; Carbohydrates: 3.8 g; Protein: 0.2 g

This is a really simple recipe with only one ingredient: sweet potato.

Fall-Themed Doggie Treats

Yield: 15–20 dog treats, depending on the chosen cutter

Ingredients:

1 medium apple, cored

1 cup canned pumpkin

5 cups oatmeal

1 egg, beaten

Directions:

1. Prepare your oven by preheating it to 400°F.

2. Use a blender to grind 4½ cups of oatmeal, then transfer it into a mixing bowl.

3. Grate the apple and add it with the oatmeal alongside the pumpkin and the egg.

4. Mix well until you get a thick dough. It should be a little sticky.

5. Prepare a surface by dusting some oatmeal on it, and roll your dough. Roll it until it reaches a thickness of about ½ inch. Use the cookie cutter of your choice and transfer the treats onto a lined baking sheet.

6. Bake the treats for about 15 minutes until they become a nice golden brown.

7. Let them cool and serve them to your dog.

8. You can store the leftover treats in the fridge in an airtight container for up to a week.

Nutritional Information Per Treat (1 of 15 total)
Calories: 121; Fat: 2.2 g; Carbohydrates: 21.9 g; Protein: 4.2 g

Instead of oats, you can use flattened rice, whole-grain flour, or quinoa flakes. You can also add banana slices or a few blueberries to make it fruitier!

Leftovers Trail Mix

Ingredients:
Vegetables (no onions)
Pieces of meat (remove flavoring if meat is seasoned)
Fruit (no raisins or grapes)
Potatoes

Directions:
1. Cut all ingredients into ½ inch pieces.
2. Spray ingredients with cooking spray.
3. Place ingredients in a food dehydrator. Alternatively, preheat the oven to 200°F and bake until the mixture is dry.

You can use leftovers to develop a great trail mix for your dog. Just look for these ingredients in your fridge to make a tasty mix that can act as a snack for your dog or to pack up if you're going for a hike.

Pumpkin Balls

Yield: 15–20 dog balls
Instructions:
2 cups whole-wheat flour
4 tablespoons water
½ cup canned pumpkin

Directions:
1. Preheat the oven to 350°F.
2. Mix pumpkin and water in a bowl. Add wheat flour and stir until dough becomes soft.
3. Take small spoonfuls of dough and roll them in your hands to form balls. It is better to wet your hands first.
4. Lightly grease a cookie sheet and place balls on it.
5. Let pumpkin balls bake for about 25 minutes until they become hard.

Nutritional Information Per Pumpkin Ball (1 of 15 total)
Calories: 63; Fat: 0.2 g; Carbohydrates: 13.4 g; Protein: 1.8 g

These pumpkin balls are great treats for your dog because they're delicious and rich in vitamin A, iron, fiber, potassium, and beta-carotene.

Apple Crunch Pupcakes

Yield: 20 pupcakes

Ingredients:

¼ cup unsweetened applesauce

4 cups whole-wheat flour

1 cup apple chips, unsweetened and dried

1 egg, beaten

2¾ cups water

Directions:

1. Preheat oven to 350°F.

2. Mix water and applesauce in a bowl. Add remaining ingredients and mix until well-blended.

3. Lightly grease muffin pans and pour the mixture inside.

4. Let bake for about 20 minutes or until edges are golden brown.

Nutritional Information (Per Treat)

Calories: 102; Fat: 0.8 g; Carbohydrates: 20.4 g; Protein: 2.9 g

This is a treat your dog will definitely love.

Coconut Dog Biscuits

Yield: 20 dog biscuits

Ingredients:

2 cups coconut flour

1 cup smooth peanut butter

1 cup coconut milk

1 tablespoon maple syrup

Directions:

1. Preheat oven to 350°F.

2. Combine peanut butter, coconut milk, and maple syrup in a bowl.

3. Add coconut flour and mix well.

4. Drop by the spoonful onto a baking sheet.

5. Bake for about 25 minutes and let cool.

Nutritional Information (Per Biscuit)

Calories: 202; Fat: 11.8 g; Carbohydrates: 19.9 g; Protein: 6.7 g

Cinnamon and Apple Cookies

Yield: 25–35 dog cookies

Ingredients:

1 cup cold water

1 teaspoon ground cinnamon

1 cup applesauce, unsweetened

2 tablespoons powdered milk

5 cups brown rice flour

½ cup coconut oil

2 eggs, beaten

Directions:

1. Combine ingredients to form a dough.

2. Refrigerate dough for 1½ hours or overnight.

3. Preheat oven to 350°F.

4. Roll dough to ½" thickness. Cut dough with a bone-shaped cookie cutter.

5. Lightly grease a cookie sheet and place cookies on it.

6. Bake for 20–25 minutes.

7. Serve once cool.

Nutritional Information Per Cookie (1 of 25 total)
Calories: 164; Fat: 5.6 g; Carbohydrates: 25.7 g; Protein: 3 g

These cookies are another treat your dog is sure to love.

Liver and Oatmeal Treats

Yield: 25–30 treats

Ingredients:

2 cups oatmeal, ground

2 pounds chicken liver, ground

4 eggs, beaten

¼ cup chicken broth

3½ cups whole-wheat flour

Directions:

1. Preheat oven to 350°F. Grease a jelly roll pan.

2. In a large bowl, mix the eggs, chicken broth, and liver.

3. Add oatmeal and flour a little at a time. Mix to form a dough.

4. Place and spread the dough on the greased pan.

5. Bake for 25–30 minutes. Test the center to make sure it's cooked all the way through.

6. Remove from oven and let cool. Loosen edges.

7. Cut into squares. Keep in refrigerator or freezer. Be sure to thaw treats before serving to your dog.

Nutritional Information Per Treat (1 of 25 total)
Calories: 160; Fat: 3.7 g; Carbohydrates: 18.2 g; Protein: 12.5 g

Sometimes your dog just wants a little extra protein. This cookie recipe is unique and delicious.

Carrot and Pumpkin Bites

Yield: 15–30 treats

Ingredients:

¼ cup carrots, shredded

1 cup whole-wheat flour

1 egg, slightly beaten

¾ cup canned pumpkin

Directions:

1. Preheat oven to 350°F.
2. Mix carrots, flour, egg, and pumpkin in a bowl.
3. Roll into small balls, placing on greased baking sheet.
4. Bake for 30–35 minutes.

Nutritional Information Per Treat (1 of 15 total)

Calories: 39; Fat: 0.4 g; Carbohydrates: 7.6 g; Protein: 1.4 g

This is another recipe that is full of nutrition for your beloved pet.

Zucchini Cookies

Yield: 12 cookies
Ingredients:
1½ cups oat flour
1 cup rolled oats
1 cup oat bran
1 teaspoon cinnamon
1 tablespoon raw honey
1 egg, lightly beaten
¾ cup nonfat milk
¼ cup zucchini, shredded

Directions:
1. Preheat oven to 350°F.
2. Combine dry ingredients in a large bowl.
3. In another bowl, beat egg and honey.
4. Add milk to dry ingredients. Add egg mixture. Blend to mix well.
5. Add zucchini and mix until well-blended.
6. Spoon batter onto a lightly greased cookie sheet. Bake for 15–20 minutes.
7. Keep frozen until ready to serve.

Nutritional Information (Per Treat)
Calories: 77; Fat: 1.6 g; Carbohydrates: 14.9 g; Protein: 3.8 g

These zucchini cookies are delicious, but they do take a little more time than the other recipes.

Cold Treat

Yield: 6 treats
Ingredients:
1 banana, mashed
1 cup apple juice
½ cup low-fat yogurt
½ cup strawberries, mashed

Directions:
1. Blend ingredients together and portion out before freezing.

Nutritional Information (Per Treat)
Calories: 55; Fat: 0.4 g; Carbohydrates: 11.5 g; Protein: 1.5 g

This is an excellent treat for the hot summer months, but it can be used year-round.

DIY Doggie Ice Cream

Yield: 8 treats
Ingredients:
1 quart plain yogurt
2 bananas
½ cup peanut butter

Directions:
1. Combine ingredients in a food processor. Pulse until smooth.
2. Pour into small plastic containers and freeze.
3. Pop out of plastic containers and serve to your dog.

Nutritional Information (Per Treat)
Calories: 208; Fat: 9.7 g; Carbohydrates: 18.5 g; Protein: 11.3 g

Everyone craves ice cream during the hot summer months, including our dogs. This recipe will leave your dog asking for more.

Tropical Treats

Yield: 12–20 treats

Ingredients:

2 cups oatmeal

1½ cups plain yogurt

1 cup cottage cheese

1 apple, cored

1 cup mango, mashed

1 tablespoon safflower oil

1 banana

Directions:

1. In a bowl, microwave oatmeal according to instructions and let cool.

2. Add apple, mango, yogurt, cheese, banana, and oil. Make sure apple and mango are thoroughly mashed before adding them.

3. Mix thoroughly and refrigerate. Serve a little bit at a time.

Nutritional Information (Per Treat)
Calories: 127; Fat: 2.9 g; Carbohydrates: 19 g; Protein: 6.4 g

Dogs like sweet mango treats, and you'll love this easy recipe.

It is important for you to consider any allergies your dog might have when preparing treats. If there's a particular ingredient you've noticed your dog has a reaction to, it would be best not to include it. If you decide to introduce something new, start by giving your dog small amounts of it to see how they react. If your dog doesn't have a problem with it, then you can feed them some more. Homemade dog treats should be kept in airtight containers before being stored in the freezer. It's always important to let the dog treats thaw for about 10–20 minutes before serving.

CHAPTER SEVEN

Recipes for Dental and Breath Treats

Homemade Dental Treats for Dogs

Yield: 5–10 treats, depending on the chosen cutter

Ingredients:

1 cup water

12 tablespoons brown rice flour

½ cup fresh mint leaves, chopped

1 tablespoon vegetable oil

1 egg, beaten

Directions:

1. Prepare your oven by preheating it to 350°F.

2. Use a food processor to mix the water, mint leaves, and vegetable oil.

3. In a separate bowl, mix the rice flour with egg. Then slowly add in the processed mix while gently stirring. Stop when the dough is no longer sticky (add more flour if needed).

4. Flour a surface and knead your dough on it. Knead it until it reaches a thickness of about ⅜ inch.

5. Use the cookie cutters of your preference to cut up the treats.

6. Place them onto a lined cooking sheet.

7. Bake for about an hour (30 minutes on each side).

8. Let the treats sit in the oven to give them a crunchy texture.

9. Serve them to your dog after they cool down.

10. Store them in the fridge, in airtight containers, for a few days.

Nutritional Information Per Treat (1 of 5 total)

Calories: 127; Fat: 4.3 g; Carbohydrates: 19 g; Protein: 3.1 g

Greenie Chewy Dental Treat

Yield: 6–8 treats, depending on the shape you choose

Ingredients:

1 cup whole-grain flour

⅓ cup of fresh mint leaves, chopped

½ cup water

⅓ cup of fat-free yogurt

1 egg, beaten

1 tablespoon vegetable oil

¼ pound ground turkey

Directions:

1. Put the yogurt in a medium bowl and mix in the vegetable oil and half the water.

2. Add in the mint, egg, oil, and turkey.

3. Mix the ingredients while slowly pouring ½ cup of flour. After that, add the rest of the water and flour.

4. Prepare a space by scattering some flour on it, and knead your dough. Make it as thick as you want and shape it however you prefer. Short, strip-like treats are good shapes because dogs can easily hold on to them and chew them. Or you can cut a ziplock bag and squeeze the dough through it to make sticks.

5. Place them onto a lined cooking sheet.

6. Bake them at 400°F for about 20 minutes until they are crispy.

7. Serve them after they cool down.

8. You can store them in the fridge, in airtight containers, for a few days.

Nutritional Information Per Treat (1 of 6 total)
Calories: 145; Fat: 5.5 g; Carbohydrates: 16.1 g; Protein: 9.8 g

Dog Breath Mints

Yield: about 20 breath mints
Ingredients:
10 crushed crackers
½ cup rolled oats
½ cup mint leaves, finely chopped
Water

Directions:
1. Mix ingredients in a bowl. Gradually add small amounts of water to the mixture until they stick together, about 4 tablespoons. Make sure the mixture is no longer crumbly before you stop.

2. Roll tiny quantities of the mixture between your hands to make small balls the size of standard mints.

3. Place dog breath mints on a sheet of waxed paper before putting them into the freezer.

4. Give your dog a few mints whenever necessary.

Nutritional Information (Per Treat)
Calories: 18; Fat: 0.5 g; Carbohydrates: 3 g; Protein: 0.5 g

Dog Breath Fresheners

Yield: 6–8 treats

Ingredients:

1 cup chickpeas, cooked

⅓ cup whole-wheat flour (more for dusting)

1 tablespoon ground flaxseeds

⅛ cup fresh parsley

1 tablespoon low-sodium chicken broth

10 fresh mint leaves

Directions:

1. Preheat oven to 300°F.

2. Combine all ingredients inside a food processor. Continue processing until chickpeas become very fine and the dough is properly mixed.

3. Roll the dough out and shape treats using cookie cutters on a lightly floured surface.

4. Bake in the oven for about 30 minutes until treats are crisp and edges are lightly browned. If you want them to be crispier, allow for more time in the oven, partly keeping the oven door open.

Nutritional Information Per Treat (1 of 6 total)
Calories: 78; Fat: 1.2 g; Carbohydrates: 13.4 g; Protein: 3.5 g

A dog that eats homemade food has a higher predisposition to developing dental plaque or having bad breath. A good idea would be to get your dog used to having their teeth brushed, with doggy toothpaste and toothbrush. If you start brushing their teeth when they are puppies, they are more likely to get used to it and accept it as adults.

If you want a simpler alternative to cooking dental treats, give your dog a nice cow bone to chew on occasionally or make some mild mint tea (unsweetened) for them to drink (for fresh breath). A few slices of pineapple will help with other unpleasant doggy smells.

Conclusion

Cooking food for your dog is easy, fun, and offers the opportunity to make your dog feel special. It also allows owners to have complete control of what their precious fur friends eat. We love our pets and want the best for them. It feels good to be 100% sure that what you are feeding your dog is as high-quality as possible.

There are plenty of recipes to try out in this book. Don't be afraid to customize them and give them a unique twist, as long as you double-check with your vet before adding anything new to your dog's diet. Remember that dogs can have allergies and that some health conditions need to be managed through a specific diet.

Also, remember that you can mix homemade food with traditional, high-quality dog food. You don't have to commit to only serving your dog home-cooked meals. You can give your dog homemade food two days a week, or you can cook treats for your lovely pooch all the time. Even if you just chop a few vegetables or fruits and mix them into your dog's kibble, that will be enough to give your dog's diet a bit of variety.

Finally, I want to thank you for reading my book. If you enjoyed the book, please share your thoughts and post a review on the book retailer's website. It would be greatly appreciated!

Best wishes,
Catalina Morris